*Happy Birthday, Consuela!*

*Tangela Y. Cooke*
*AKA*
*Cookie*
*9/10/06*

# Cookie's Corner
## Same Block, Different Avenue

### Tangela Yvette Cooke

1663 Liberty Drive, Suite 200
Bloomington, Indiana 47403
(800) 839-8640
www.AuthorHouse.com

© 2005 Tangela Yvette Cooke All Rights Reserved.

No part of this book may be reproduced, stored in a retrieval system, or transmitted by any means without the written permission of the author.

First published by AuthorHouse 10/25/05

ISBN: 1-4208-7898-0 (sc)

Printed in the United States of America
Bloomington, Indiana

This book is printed on acid-free paper.

Cover Design by Tangela Y. Cooke

Dedicated to my Mom
I miss you so much.

*For all have sinned and come
short of the glory of God.*
-Romans 3:23

# Contents

| | |
|---|---|
| **Preface** | **xi** |
| **Introduction** | **xv** |
| **Candy House** | **1** |
| S.I. | 3 |
| This Skin I'm in | 4 |
| The Fairytale | 5 |
| Theft by Deception – A Victim's Story | 6 |
| I Fell in Love | 8 |
| Love Is Blind | 9 |
| Secret Love | 10 |
| A Moment of Reflection | 11 |
| Hell Has No Fury… | 12 |
| Mad Cow | 13 |
| I-WOEMAN'S R.Q. | 14 |
| T'was the Night Before the 36th Anniversary of the day I Was Born | 15 |
| **Invisible Church** | **17** |
| No Love for Cheaters | 19 |
| Bitch | 21 |
| Prelude to an Ultimatum | 23 |
| Man Up | 24 |
| None | 25 |
| A Sober Message | 26 |
| Mass Confusion | 27 |
| Psalm of a Single Woman | 29 |
| Joy Ride | 30 |
| Dear Tamar | 31 |
| Race Relations | 33 |
| **The Guy Next Door** | **35** |
| Victor | 37 |
| No Heart Feelings | 38 |
| Specious | 39 |

| | |
|---|---|
| Whew | 40 |
| Ulterior Motives | 41 |
| His Ideology | 42 |
| A Bedtime Story | 43 |
| He Kissed Me | 44 |
| Tell Me Something Good | 45 |
| Noncommittal Crap | 46 |
| Crazy Cancer | 47 |
| MICHAEL | 48 |

## 69th Street and Secks Court    51

| | |
|---|---|
| How Sweet | 53 |
| Lucky #7 | 54 |
| Silly | 55 |
| Just the Pussy –a Dog's Perspective | 56 |
| Out of Cervix | 57 |
| Flesh Speaks, Intellect Reasons and Spirit Commands | 58 |

## 2nd Stoetry & Still Bldg.    61

| | |
|---|---|
| COOKE UNIVERSITY-SCHOOL OF TYCOLOGY | 63 |
| Beauty and the Beast 2003 | 64 |
| The Sax Man and Ms. Filharmonica | 65 |
| Jamaic'n Me Crazy Too | 66 |
| Seven Miles | 67 |
| Toxic | 68 |
| Determined | 69 |
| What if… | 70 |

## Pundit's Playground    71

| | |
|---|---|
| Living the Dream | 73 |
| Forget About the Funeral | 74 |
| I Think Very Deeply: Processing | 75 |
| I Think Very Deeply: Deprogramming | 76 |
| MY LOCKS | 77 |
| Quality Time | 78 |
| Mirror, Mirror | 79 |
| Love AT LARJ | 80 |
| ArboREAL Experience | 81 |

Empirical 82
Hello... Children First 83

# Memory Lane 85

Autobio Poem – Age 15 87
All in the Opened Doors to the Future (1984) 88
Autobio Poem – Age 17 89
Just Say No! (1987) 90
Forecast (1989) 91

# Home Sweet Home 93

To a Woman's Heart 95
The Take Off 96
Prolific 97
Kismet 98
Her Written Soliloquy 100
SM 102
Untitled 104
My Soul's Creation 105

# Dead End 107

Hurricane T (ending in A) (1987) 109
You're Right (1988) 110
Innocent Brown Goddess (1997) 111
(1998) 113
(2002) 114
Sober Poetry (2003) 115

# Preface

*Cookie's Corner* started off as a physical place. From the ages of 15 to 18 I lived in a cozy house located at 1270 NW 72nd Street in the heart of Liberty City, Miami, Florida. In this perfect rectangle of a house were four bedrooms. There was a bedroom situated at each angle. I named my bedroom *Cookie's Corner*.

*Cookie's Corner* was my thinking place, study room, sublet or home within a home, retreat from my family and escape from the world. As a teenager, I would shut my door, clean and/or organize my room and write. In fact, *Cookie's Corner* is where the majority of my poems were created as an adolescent.

At the age of 23, I left Liberty City and didn't look back (except on occasion to visit relatives or to tour the city to see if it had developed or improved).

*Cookie's Corner* is no longer a fixture or physical dwelling place. It has become a mental and spiritual place that dwells inside me. It's my state of mind, my consciousness and my Soul. Ever since I uprooted from Liberty City, *Cookie's Corner* goes wherever I go.

Everyone is now welcome to visit *Cookie's Corner*, to see how or what I think. However, I recommend that you go through *Tangible Times* first.

Tangela Y. Cooke
October 21, 2003

# Cookie's Corner
## Same Block, Different Avenue

*There is a time for everything, and a season
for every activity under heaven:*

*a time to be born and a time to die,
a time to plant and a time to uproot,
a time to kill and a time to heal,
a time to tear down and a time to build,
a time to weep and a time to laugh,
a time to mourn and a time to dance,
a time to scatter stones and a time to gather them,
a time to embrace and a time to refrain,
a time to search and a time to give,
a time to keep and a time to throw away,
a time to tear and time to mend,
a time to be silent and a time to speak
a time to love and a time to hate,
a time for peace and a time for war.*

-Ecclesiastes 3:1-8

# Introduction

I thank God for yet another blessing. I am so excited to announce the birth of my second brainchild, *Cookie's Corner*. I am so proud of my baby, yet she also humbles me. Coming up with a subtitle presented me with a challenge. However, I was able to narrow my choices to Where Every Woman Lives, A Poetic Lifetime and Same Block, Different Avenue. I believe all three were good choices for different reasons. Where Every Woman Lives is my play on Chaka Khan's song "I'm Every Woman." I considered it because I am every woman (i.e., sister, aunt, friend, teacher, evangelist, the woman scorned, etcetera.) A Poetic Lifetime was an option because, like the movies on the popular cable station- Lifetime, many of my poems appeal to women. But only one subtitle was sufficient.

I selected Same Block, Different Avenue because metaphorically speaking, block and avenue represent my mind and line of thinking respectively. I also wanted to stick to the theme for titles of each chapter that happen to be named after places in a neighborhood.

*Cookie's Corner* contains poetic imitations of life- real and imagined. Like most art, my poetry is filled with emotion- love, passion, anger, and the whole shebang. Honestly, I didn't realize that I was such a drama queen (in my writing) until after I finished reading *Cookie's Corner*... talk about Lifetime, or soap operas for that matter. But don't get me wrong, I enjoyed every moment of it.

I can go on and on rambling about the conception, delivery and naming of my baby, but I'll spare you all of the details. Anyway, I'd rather you see her, hold her, and get to know her for yourself. I'm sure you'll like her too. In the meantime I'd like to thank you in advance for picking up *Cookie's Corner*. Thank you! Enjoy!

God bless,

## Tangela Y. Cooke

Sunday, December 19, 2004
Atlanta, Georgia
10:41 p.m.

# Candy House

*Someone was hurt before you; wronged before you; hungry before you; frightened before you; beaten before you; humiliated before you; raped before you; yet, someone survived.*
-Maya Angelou

## S.I.

I observed a silver intruder demand my attention
In a restricted area, a private community,
Not open to the public.
(Although a visitor would find it rather enchanting)

This intruder beckoned me.
She spoke in a gentle, yet wavering tone, announcing
That time is fleeting and shortly my strong,
Youthful community would be exiting their prime.

As the crowd of dark natives, parted and then curtsied
(as a symbol of respect for the elder intruder)
She stepped forward and reminded me that
"Change will come."

She made no apologies for her not so subtle appearance
and insisted that it was my own ignorance that alarmed me.

She explained that life is a process of growth and change.
She emphasized that it was important for me, the head of the community,
to understand that no matter what shade or age:
dark, light, silver, old or young,
we all grow or just change.

Her last words still echo in my mind,
"One day soon, you and all the natives, will look like me."
She then bowed gracefully.

And I immediately ejected her from the community.

*Tangela Yvette Cooke*

# This Skin I'm in

And the cellulite
is the result of a man not loving me
it's the result of my foiled attempt
to become who he wanted me to be

Though before we started dating
he said I was fine
he adored my long, sexy legs
and my perfectly small waistline

And after the honeymoon period
model-fine met its end
sexy and slim was out
round and "voluptuous"- the trend

Like a habitual man-pleaser,
I was silly, insane
I inhaled Krispe Kreme doughnuts
and guzzled weight gain

Stopped going to the gym
due to his indirect advice,
"A man doesn't want to feel a hard woman,
he wants a soft body, soft thighs"

After confronting his new image
in my silver-coated glass
I cursed the curvaceous woman
with lumpy thighs and puckered ass

I ignored my man's wishes
and his comments about my weight
said hello to self-love
called the gym, made a date

Had to remind myself
to appreciate the skin I'm in
and accept the way that God made me
strong, beautiful, and thin.

# The Fairytale

Love and marriage
marriage and sex
can be so simple,
yet so complex.

Sex is a love problem
and a marriage solution.
Women are confused by love
after sex's execution.

He loves me, so we made love-
although he might think it was just sex.
He makes two simple synonyms
seem so complex.

He'll marry me because he loves me.
He loves me because we had sex.
Such a simple deduction,
yet for him, it's so complex.

Love leads to sex-
that is no illusion.
More sex after marriage
is the logical conclusion.

*Tangela Yvette Cooke*

# Theft by Deception – A Victim's Story

He walked into my life
with the worst of intentions.
He saw me
and the only things that he could see
were legs and a vagina
to divide and conquer.

He didn't know that a woman's
brain, heart and vagina are interrelated
and interconnected parts.
He didn't know that when a man loved one,
he loved them all
and when he screwed over one, he …
well, you get the picture.

When he met me
I was happy, independent, virtuous
and positive.
I was at peace –
no man, no stuff and no drama.
My mind, body and Soul
were in equilibrium.

He saw me.
He made a choice to approach me.
He asked for my number.
He pretended to want to know me
and then he screwed me (over and over again).
He disappeared
without cause, explanation,
and even saying good-bye.

... and me,
well, I'm left feeling
demoralized, defiled, denigrated and degraded.
I'm off-balance and
I (reluctantly) can almost relate to and
identify with Alex Forrest and Brandi Web.

Why did I allow him
to come into my life?
It's too late now.
I let him inside
and he stole my peace
(amongst other things)
and my three-organ system
incessantly communicates my losses to me.

*Tangela Yvette Cooke*

# I Fell in Love

I fell in love with a possibility and
all I had to do
was like its means.

I fell in love
with the potential for
falling in love,
having fun, and
creating artistic expressions
with someone.

I fell in love with
an expectation of achieving
loyalty, faithfulness, and
a life-long friendship, and
partnership.

I fell in love with
the idea that we
were compatible.

I fell in love with a chance
that I had found
my Soul mate
who had all the attributes
of a man I would be destined to marry.

I fell in love with
false certainty
that his character was unblemished.

I fell in love because of manufactured intuition.

# Love Is Blind

I can see clearly now
the love is gone.
I can't believe I dated
Dr. Burns, a troll and
a gnome.

It's funny how he appears
hot and handsome
when you are together
you love his eyes
adore his smile
and the attraction is like- forever.

But when the honeymoon is over,
and he changes his colors
Mr. Hyde is bound to appear.
He starts looking like Homer
and acting like a jerk
so the picture becomes clear.

Yeah, love is like a drug
it has some of the same effects
and it can distort the vision of the beholder.
She'll think her hulk is a hunk
or her toad is a prince,
despite the truth that is shown her.

*Tangela Yvette Cooke*

# Secret Love

I'm placing my love for him
on my cerebral shelf-
don't want to get
ahead of myself.

I'm placing more
in the corner of my heart.
I refuse to chase him away
or make a false start.

I'm placing some
in the back of my mind-
don't want to misplace it,
not this kind.

I'm placing a bit
in the pit of my belly.
I must not reveal it.
Love might seem scary.

I'm placing traces
in the lining of my Soul-
smoothing out gaps
and filling in holes.

I'm hiding my love for him-
keeping it safe
and I will reveal it in time.
I will show it my way.

# A Moment of Reflection

At 35
My desire for marriage
Has greatly declined
Just like a 50-year-old man's
Stamina and sex drive

Why?

It just happened over time
There's really nothing
Or no one to blame
And I love my life
Just the same

*Tangela Yvette Cooke*

# Hell Has No Fury...

Yes, I destroyed our sofa and love seat.

You'll never provide comfort for another woman's behind
on something we bought.

... and your sound system and CD collection-
I threw them across the apartment.
Since they didn't have eyes,
they flew into the walls and
were destroyed beyond recognition.

But they're no worse off than my heart.

... and the television-
it met its fate too.
You'll never entertain another female with that set.

By the way, I politely tossed all of your other treasures
in the trash can.
I figured the love, honor, respect and loyalty that you showed me
needed some company.

... and our pictures-
I didn't bother to deface them, I just tore them up.
It's the least I could do to help you
phase me and our memories out of your life.

I left you the beds.
It would take too much for me to damage them.
Besides, you've already tainted them.

Finally, I didn't touch your clothes.
Through all of this I've managed to keep
my sense of reason, rationale and logic.
Since I'm leaving with only my clothes,
you should have yours too.

Now we can start over equally.

# **Mad Cow**

Time and time again I satisfy your needs
And give you milk for free
Yet you take me for granted, although I share my teats-
Giving Grade A...unselfishly

Prodded and pulled, I'm seeing red- you milk me
But nothing comes from your pocket
Either give me the farm or give up meat
Before this heifer comes off the market

*Tangela Yvette Cooke*

# I-WOeMAN'S R.Q.

If the Red Sea is the beginning of womanhood,
is the Dead Sea the end?

Since Eve was the first to disobey God,
is woman the mother of sin?

If the womb differentiates man from woman-
and the male from female, the fetus,

does this mean if woman and I can't or don't procreate,
mankind does not need us?

If God created woman to be man's helpmate,
but she's single with no prospects,

does this mean she hasn't fulfilled her reason for being
and she's a purposeless defect?

If a woman was blessed with the possibility of having children,
but had no blessed opportunity,

does this mean she's incomplete
because of her childlessness destiny?

If a woman totally loves herself
more than any other,

can the love-yourself-first theory be cast as psychobabble,
when love's not reciprocated by her lover?

If a woman reflects an air of *yes, I care,*
even when she feels the world doesn't share her view,

Should she step down turn her smile into a frown,
and with hold her love from you?

# T'was the Night Before the 36th Anniversary of the day I Was Born

I don't want to close my eyes just yet
I'm not ready to end another year
I don't want the short and long hand to hint
that menopause is near

I don't want to blow out another candle
I'm not ready to mourn my youth
I don't want Hallmark cards or presents-
conceal my birth certificate, hide the truth

I don't want to enumerate the annals since my birth
Each new day is a reason to celebrate for me
I don't want to have that single event or miracle
counted each year for eternity

I have accepted getting older
because with aging there is no election
It's each damn number with its stereotype attached
that is the impetus for my "Happy Birthday" rejection

My happy birthday happened one time
let's not stop and rewind... let it go
Let's just live a Happy Lifetime
by letting our Happy Days flow

# Invisible Church

*Know ye not that ye are the temple of God, and that the Spirit of God dwelleth in you?*
-1 Corinthians 3:16-17

# No Love for Cheaters

I believe in doing the wise thing
and I'm not quoting a line I heard.
I have zero tolerance for cheating
because any tolerance is absurd.

Why have sex with another person,
who's not your partner or your wife?
Why even bother to make a commitment
if you want to live a single life?

Sharing their saliva, their bodily secretions
and all that sin-ergy.
Killing their spirits, their happily ever afters
with your trifling adultery.

Why can't you be monogamous?
Why ... so hard to satisfy?
Why do you tell each one *I love you*?
Why must they live your lie?

You make me sick; you're nasty–
to think of what folks do in bed.
You're going back and forth between women–
not thinking with the right head.

God gave women intuition
and a large dose of common sense.
Yet one pleads desperation
and the other, ignorance.

You mock marriage, manhood and mores.
She has no self-respect:
two selfish, ungodly, poor displays
of immorality at its best.

Using each other for sex and things,
wasting valuable time
messing up lives, lessons and families
with behaviors by no means sublime.

*Tangela Yvette Cooke*

Some grown-ups need to grow up!
So their children will live right, not wrong.
'Cause if mama and someone else's husband keeps up
this cycle will just go on.

# Bitch

Down
Girl!
Yeah,
I'm talkin' to you.
Will you ever use your *will*
To stop doin' the things you do?

A bitch doesn't care
Or can't discern
The pedigrees that she takes.
She'll secret pheromones,
Wag her tail and whoever sniffs
She'll mate.

Don't think just because
you use protection
You're a clever fox.
Trust that latex
Won't *protect* your heart
Once your past
Begins to bark.

So stop actin'
like a jackal in heat,
hunchin' anything with legs.
Stop behavin'
like an unleashed freak
who's too horny to use her head.

So technically
you're not a whore
or so called *lady* of the streets
because you voluntarily
share your tail with
every dog you meet.

*Tangela Yvette Cooke*

But what's to be said
about humping to be humped
versus doin' it for the bread ...
either way –
lie with dogs – get pups or fleas
even worse- a bitch can end up dead.

# Prelude to an Ultimatum

Perhaps one day
you'll stop viewing and casting me
as your insignificant other
and accept and recognize me as
your girlfriend…

and when you start to value me as
a necessity and not just
a luxury or commodity
I will gain importance in your life.

Hopefully, in days to come,
marriage and I will become
your goal and priority.

*Tangela Yvette Cooke*

# Man Up

Man up my brother.
Keep a job, make a plan.
Don't adopt your daddy's character flaws
by being a deadbeat to your clan.

I can only be objective,
since I haven't walked in your shoes.
But we know YOU'RE NOT YOUR DADDY
so start being true to you.

You weren't "born to be this way."
Your dad's way is not His will.
Step up to the plate.
Be a better man.
Make your music, but pay the bills.

Seven Souls are counting on you
for more than your love and presence per se.
Show your children how a man and father should be–
by antiquating the deadbeat of yesterday.

# None

I am a None because I can't see *straight*
and the DL brothers were the catalyst for my state.

I am a None because I've had enough
of games, noncommittal men and other trifling stuff.

I am None because I can do without
this hyper-sexual explosion and its HIV/AIDS fallout.

I am a None because I have all I need:
a strong mind, great health and a God-centered creed.

I am a None because I'm not desperate, I'm blessed.
I want a God-fearing man and I won't settle for less.

Please know that I am not a traditional nun.
My convent is my home and my vows are through His Son.

And this repentant one has had some but has promised to abstain.
Until I can follow the precepts of His Word– a None, I will remain.

*Tangela Yvette Cooke*

# A Sober Message

I don't have to consume spirits
to let you hear it.

I don't have to drink rum
just to have fun.

I don't have to drink wine
to relax my mind.

I don't have to get drunk
to dance, party or get *crunk*.

I don't have to be a lush
to react to my lust.

I don't have to imbibe
to survive or stay alive.

I don't have to drink alcohol. Want to know why?
The Creator has blessed me with a natural high.

## **Mass Confusion**

Using the birth of Christ
as a guise
to begrudgingly give gifts and
glorify
greed and gluttony

Confusing Christmas
with Krismas
to celebrate
gift-giving or
Giftsmust

with stories of
Kris Kringle
on Christmas

what about our savior
who died for our sins,
crucified on the cross
with nails in both hands

Was it Santa Clause
or Satan's Clause
that provided for
the red suit and
the fat, jolly man

to climb down a hot, narrow
chimney in the midst
of winter
to deliver presents
or Lucifer's presence
to lighten the hearts of children
and capture their Souls
by giving material things– not love

Using the birth or mass
of Christ
as a reason to spend bread,
have a feast or get fed
and drink wine
to get drunk

don't forget to
take the presents
out of the trunk

and you say
"Jesus is the reason for the season"

Then where's the
love and the
ho, ho, holy spirit on December 25$^{th}$
Maybe it's wrapped
up under the Givemust tree or
beneath the mistletoe

Giftmas-
formerly known as Christmas
is just one of the
ramifications
of transforming a
pagan holiday
and renaming it
in celebration of
His birthday

# Psalm of a Single Woman

Deliver me from temptation, LORD, for
I am weak.
Feed my spirit, LORD, so that my flesh
    does not hunger.
I am lustful.
        How long, O LORD, until you take away
            my physical desires.
Remove my sinful thoughts, LORD, and keep
    my temple sacred.
You are the lover of my Soul, LORD,
    please sustain me.

                      Amen

*Tangela Yvette Cooke*

# Joy Ride

Just give me
a fast car
and a phallic toy-
I don't need another boyfriend
to bring me joy.

Let me cruise
on automatic pilot
(translation-
God is in control).
Until he's man enough
to not fornicate,
let this single,
holy roller roll.

# Dear Tamar

To my sister,
        who has confided in me-
                *the* rape
I know my tears,
        outrage and
                compassion
won't help
        you
                escape
the murder
        of a piece
                of your body and Soul,
the invisible gapes
        that leave you
                not feeling whole
and the theft
        of your virtue
                no, you're not to blame
for his evil,
        heinous act-
                that has left you in pain
all I can do
        is pray
                (as you do)
that you're
        able to sleep,
                be strong and stay true ...
to think – Jesus died
        for that monster-
                the sins of fallen man
the rape
        was an abomination
                and a violation of God's plan...
He loves you
        more than we love you
                and He *will* make a way
for you to be at peace
        and sleep well
                each night after you pray

*Tangela Yvette Cooke*

and that monster...
                he'll surely get his
                              no crime goes unpunished
just have faith
                that He'll heal
                            and restore you
and watch
                how your spirit
                            continues to flourish

# Race Relations

During my first serious relationship
I had to compete with his parents, friends,
bars and nightclubs.

I came in last place.

During my second serious relationship
I had to compete with his children, career,
the news and sports television.

I came in last place.

In my present serious relationship
I have to compete with his dominion,
yet I receive his full, undivided attention.

I am a winner.

# The Guy Next Door

*As water reflects a face, so a man's heart reflects the man.*
Proverbs 21:19

# Victor

Defeated by self
I hide behind my name.
For I am only a shell of a man.
My spine weakened by the strength of time.
My mind has morphed into mush after abuse by my lies or mistrust.
My heart is just not there, for I don't feel love and I don't care.

My life is a paradox,
My name, a misnomer.

*Tangela Yvette Cooke*

# No Heart Feelings

I let one man
who behaved cowardly-
demonstrating neglect and disregard for me
and revealing an utter lack of sensibility,
affect my peace and mentality
by provoking scorn and hostility.

I let one man
attack my dignity
by involving unneeded autocracy
and unnecessary police authority
despite my convictions about misology
and his miscreant acts and treatment of me.

I let one man
get the best of me
evoking my misandry and misogamy
after he showed blatant disrespect for me
with excuses without apologies
and no heart feelings, just apathy.

… and now I must *let*
this one man see
I won't let him have *this* power over me
or emasculate men haphazardly
because he projected his simple-mindedness unto me.
I rebuke him and his negativity.

# Specious

He was drop-dead gorgeous.
This man was drop-dead fine.
He had a drop-dead sense of style
(forgot to focus on his mind).
He had a drop-dead personality,
not to mention a drop dead life.
But his drop-dead left hook
had me reaching for a knife.
Now I wish he'd just drop dead.

*Tangela Yvette Cooke*

# Whew

I'm sorry it did not work out
but I did care for you.
Looks like it wasn't meant to be.
So, all I can say is – whew.

It's a blessing that neither one of us was hurt.
Our breakup *was* overdue.
At least this brother did not dog you out.
But all I can say is-whew.

We didn't bring a child into our drama.
We skipped the old, borrowed and blue.
Please know that we can still be friends.
For now, my heart and mind says – whew.

# Ulterior Motives

There are plenty of men
ready and willing to do
the kinds of things
that you like to do
to yield to your expectations
and make your wishes come true.

Take heed – keep in mind that
what he's willing to do
is probably to benefit him
more than benefit you;
his motives might just be
to make his fantasy come true.

What he does for you
will overshadow the clue
that what he ultimately wants
is to do the do
with you.

*Tangela Yvette Cooke*

# His Ideology

For him,
compatibility
had everything to do with
occasional and/or casual sex
and nothing to do with
commonalties.

For him,
control,
not communication
and compromise
was the key
to commitment.

For him,
passion
meant fulfilling
her physical needs
by way of pleasing himself
even if it could be construed by her
as perfunctory.

# A Bedtime Story

I finally know a man
with whom I'm compatible with in bed.
He doesn't mind when I use his chest
as a pillow for my head.

I can toss my stuffed bear on the floor
and snuggle with him on the sheets;
and when his warm skin touches mine
I have no trouble falling asleep.

He doesn't resort to the aft play-
cuddle, push and roll.
When he's down for the count and I'm knocked out
our bodies still feel whole.

I can't believe it. For six to eight straight hours
his body touches mine.
He doesn't mind spooning or my head on his biceps
or when our bodies are just aligned.

I finally know a man with whom I'm compatible
and I'm not referring to overrated sex.
I'm talking French kisses, lots of affection
and tongue massages on the neck.

# He Kissed Me

I asked him what was on his mind and he kissed me.

His kiss
rendered me helpless.

His kiss
left me speechless.

I want to believe that
his kiss
was his way of saying,
"I miss you,
I want you,
I need you,
and I like you,
so let's get to know each other better."

His kiss
not only dissolved my inhibitions,
but also melted the ice that encased or
protected my heart.

His kiss
made me hopeful.

He kissed me
and I didn't want him to stop kissing me,
but he stopped
and then he left.

He kissed me
and the impression
from his lips
remains on mine

and secretly-I know
his kiss was the answer
that communicated, "Sex."

# Tell Me Something Good

I met a guy
who was interested in my mind-
my educational background,
my opinions,
and my perspective on some of life's questions.
I was impressed
and this was something good.

I met a man
who was curious about my body-
my fitness goals,
my efforts to stay in shape,
and my overall health.
I was touched
and this was something good.

I met a person
who was attracted to my spirit-
my positive energy and
my relationship with God.
He encouraged me to take in the word
each and everyday.
His attitude was refreshing
and this was good.

Now ain't that something.

*Tangela Yvette Cooke*

# Noncommittal Crap

When I see you again
save the love- give dap
cuz I had a chance
to process... focus and recap
shedding my chastity belt
was my impetuous mishap
that left me feeling used
after your not ready for... rap
and made me want to
replace a kiss with a slap
cuz you had me chasing a fantasy...
lost- without a map
so I had to swallow the truth
and take a power nap
to meditate about reality-
how your truth hurts with a zap
a reminder to keep 'em close
don't make 'em clap
or just leave them up
and close the gap
and just sit on the sofa
not on your lap
so I will be neither your lover
nor your sap
'cause your second rejection
has made me quite apt
I've learned to say *no* too
'cause I'm not ready for crap.

## Crazy Cancer

He bases his behavior on the zodiac
or astrology, the moon and dreams
He claims to be clairvoyant and a mystic
who knows when things aren't what they seem

He's a child of Eros and emotion-
allowing feelings to be his measure
of love, life and relationships
and the principle of what brings him pleasure

He confuses tradition with his individual expectations
and his need to feel secure
He runs the gamut of driving her away
in a misguided effort to allure

This crab has a Pavlovic pinch
he seeks to subliminally control
and practices psychiatry without a license
as a means to define her role

Quiet and confused he laughs when not amused
but wants to be taken seriously
If I was to foretell his horoscope in tomorrow's paper
I'd say- let the crazy cancer be

# MICHAEL

In retrospect,
it's not farfetched to think
that-
perhaps he was my guardian angel;
and like steps in a family,
he and I created a
Familial
Relationship
Intrinsically
Entailing
No
DNA,
Since
His
Initial
Presence in my life.

In him I confided all and everything
and in great detail.

Besides God and myself,
he knew me better and
knows more about me than anyone else.

He was there for me during my late teens and
shared all of my trying twenties.

With him, I can always be my
real, true, genuine, authentic and sincere
silly or serious self.

I've had more fun,
adventures,
explorations, and
experimentation
with him than anyone thus far.

He's
loved, hurt, helped, taught, saved, supported and protected me.

He and I have been through it all
together: storms, hurricanes,
and other human disasters.

Our bond has withstood
the tests of time.

... and no matter what he does,
I'll always love him.

# 69th Street and Secks Court

*Very few lasting relationships are made in bed.
Fantasies may begin and end there; true love does not.*
-Dr. Harold Bessell

# How Sweet

I'm lookin' for a man
who has a weakness for chocolate
not vanilla, strawberry
or a Napoleon composite
take a slice of the cake
that my mama baked
finish all of my cookie crumbs
slow, gentle-like – not all thumbs
nibble my Hershey's kisses
taste my Tootsie Roll Cherry Pop
take your time and savor the flavor
stroke the bottom, lick the top
don't crave chocolate flavored mocha
just let it pass your lips
feel the warmth inside
it won't scorch you,
no sloppy slurps, take sips
once I've quenched your thirst for mocha
and you've turned over the cup
cut the brownies that I've made for you
all of *this* will fill you up.

*Tangela Yvette Cooke*

# Lucky #7

The inevitable happened yesterday-
That is you inside of me.
It was too late to deliver me from temptation
or Immortality.

First… our acquaintance in the parking lot;
Second… your screenplay and poetry readings;
Third… drinks at Intermezzo's
Left me psycho-sexually ceding…

There were no profound discussions between us
or exchanges about our pasts.
There was small talk with light laughter and conversation
and what happened next, happened fast.

It started out with innocent kissing.
It led to touching on the bed.
Then disrobing became a necessity
because of erotica on the head.

Three times – you revealed your prowess at seduction,
Four times- you used your charm, and
Your sexiness, virility, strength and intellect
just happened to be tattooed on your arm.

# Silly

You're a piece of candy with a booty,
an appetizer at the most.
He doesn't see you in his tomorrow.
Today is his party
and you're the host.

He's leading you on baby girl.
Your so-called courtship is a guise.
He's just keeping himself occupied-
playing it safe
and being wise.

No – you won't meet his parents
or be an influence in his life.
No – you won't pique his interest.
He's not looking
for a wife.

Yes – you've been bamboozled.
It's round four – panties down.
He's keepin' your relā
on the down low.
He's playin' you for a clown.

… another penis for your memoirs.
Shove the door – bones are coming out.
… another lesson you'll surely repeat
until you learn
what they're about.

Don't kid yourself, you're not naive:
after sex you don't feel muddy.
Check yourself.
Don't get it twisted.
You're just his interest-free cut-buddy.

*Tangela Yvette Cooke*

# Just the Pussy – a Dog's Perspective

Let me be your personal call boy
or be your special friend:
a friend with unlimited benefits
and a love-life,
let's pretend.

We can eat dinner, hang out,
or kick it under the sun.
We can do a movie,
drink and chill
I just want to have fun.

I want a no-strings-attached relationship.
I'm not pursuing a one-night-stand.
I don't intend to ask for your parents' blessings
to crown the index finger
on your left hand.

We don't have to exchange Hallmark cards
or let things get too mushy.
I'm not searching for my Soul mate
I'll settle for
just the pussy.

## Out of Cervix

I've had
more sex
than a little bit.
After so many men,
you'd think
I'd quit.
I've learned that
a promiscuous life style
ain't worth spit.
So I'm no longer
virtuously
broken down -
just closed
and celibate.

*Tangela Yvette Cooke*

# Flesh Speaks, Intellect Reasons and Spirit Commands

Beyond her
soft lips
I can hear
and feel
her reverberate,
"Let him in,"
in sotto voce.
With empathetic insight
I try to
reason with her-
let her know
that he's not
worth it-
remind her that
he's been
in and out…
too many times
already.
"He chose to stay out."
And even though
she wants him
to remain (in her life)
till death…,
he won't.
So keep him out.
She begins
to weep to the point of saturation
and from moistened,
trembling lips
and a throbbing core
she pleads
to give him
a soft, warm
placating place
to put

or rest his head.
I tell her,
"Pull yourself together,
dry it up
and close your mouth."
This (feeling), too, shall pass.

# 2nd Stoetry & Still Bldg.

*Imagination is the eye of the soul.*
-Joseph Jouber

# COOKE UNIVERSITY- SCHOOL OF TYCOLOGY

Cooke University's School of Tycology
was founded in January 1969.
Like the Ivies' curriculum,
this great institution challenges the mind.

If you're not God-fearing, confident and secure,
there's no need to apply.
Men of outstanding character, integrity and standard
should browse our syllabi.

Our school offers an array of studies
embodied in Tangela Yvette Cooke.
If you're a serious candidate seeking a bright future-
C.U. is where you should look.

A man who's grounded, true to himself and God
has met three admissions requirements.
But he must also be mentally, emotionally and spiritually sound
and very intelligent.

Your time at C.U. will be an excellent investment
and if you're accepted, you'll see.
Just be prepared to commit to and study
all levels of Tycology.

*Tangela Yvette Cooke*

# Beauty and the Beast 2003

Quasimodo was not his name
though he was like the Hunchback
of Notre Dame:

Long torso, gigantic head,
a hairy back, long arms,
short legs,

a massive, brown Hulk,
with crimson, coiled hair,
a distinctive voice
and Victor Hugo's flair.

Yet this beautiful, brown princess
was neither frightened nor repulsed
by the beast –
this tall, dwarf-like creature.

She embraced him,
while and without wearing regal,
rose-colored glasses.

However, the beast,
A carnal conundrum – ungracious and wild,
was true to its form.
He was no prince and there was no happily ever after.

# The Sax Man and Ms. Filharmonica

*dedicated to W. Henley Varner*

The sax man plays the saxophone
and it sounds crisp and clear,
but he doesn't have to play for just anyone
now that Filharmonica's here.

He's known for two major compositions,
Cool and Jazzy are their names.
Playing music in the key of life
this virtuoso sustains.

Yes, he can play that saxophone
and it's as sensual as making love.
Melodious, rhythmic, seductive and smooth
its harmony creates lots of

Music so strong and gentle-
it's an exciting contradiction.
His mouth-breath-reed collaboration
causes terminal sax addiction.

It massages the mind and penetrates the Soul-
the body can't help but lose it.
Fingers snap while feet tap
...feel the vibe and groove it.

Adagio to Allegro - crescendo to diminuendo
the sax man carries the tune.
So soulful, hypnotic, soothing, and erotic-
the end would come too soon.

Play that saxophone man,
played low and soft causes healing.
Play that saxophone man,
played loud and hard it's still appealing.
Just ask Filharmonica

*Tangela Yvette Cooke*

# Jamaic'n Me Crazy Too
*summary of my 2003 vacation*

Caribbean breezes on the South Coast
Blue Mountains, blue skies, but I won't boast
      and ganja, me no want it

Seven-mile beaches with soft, white sand
Beautiful African people, inhabiting inland
      but cannabis, me no want it

Dunn's River Falls, Rick's Café
An Island Safari and tubing all day
      but hemp, me no want it

Red, black and yellow – displayed with pride
British oppression – too hard to hide
      and weed, me no want it

Taxis (no problem), seafood and more
Bob Marley, reggae and markets galore
      but holy herb, me no want it

Natural waterfalls, palm trees, partying strips
Unsolicited tour guides expecting their tips
      but marijuana, me no want it

On a cliff or at sunset, me no want it
      Feelin' hot, hot, hot, but me no want it
            And everything's Irie, so me no want it

# Seven Miles
*-An internal conversation on the treadmill*

My mind told me:
> Our legs are giving out.
> We are tired. Walk.
> We cannot do this.
> Why are we doing this? STOP!

My body told me:
> Because we eat right,
> because we drink enough water,
> because we stretch to maintain our flexibility, and
> because we treat our body like the temple that it is -
> we have the strength of an elephant. RUN!

My spirit told me:
> "We can do all things through Christ who gives us strength."
> "Now unto him that is able to do exceedingly abundantly
> above all that we ask or think, according to the power that
> worketh in us."
> "Fear not. Have faith." RUN!

My spirit insisted that "a heart at peace is life to the body."
So we honored God with our body. We ran.

During the last mile, I slowed down.
Just when we were about to concede or stop running,
my mind whispered that we can do it.

Then my mind confessed aloud:
> He made our body, so run and feel healthier.
> He paid for our body, so run and look better.
> He's indwelt in us, so run and live longer.

So we picked up the pace and continued to run.
We ran wholeheartedly physically, spiritually
as well as mentally and we completed our seven miles in one accord.

*Tangela Yvette Cooke*

# Toxic

I confronted your mistress the other day.
Since we skipped the introductions- I'll unaffectionately call her Slim.
I gave Slim the once-over, sized her up and
concluded that although she is sexy, slender and petite,
she doesn't have anything on me.
I take that back- she has you.
Slim assured me that you weren't giving her up any time soon.
She added that she has you rapped around her finger- so to speak.
You can't believe that she respects you.
She says that you're full of hot air and I know that's not a compliment.
Hard to believe that you're still with her even after she threatened
your life.
Yes, she told me everything.
Slim even claims that you'll die for her.
She said that she has you whipped-
and that you can't let go because she gives you oral pleasure.
Don't I satisfy you?
Lord, I don't understand it.
She ain't no good and your relationship with her can't be healthy.
That girl is toxic… and you'd sacrifice all that you have for her.

## **Determined**

pushing my peds through Peachtree Park-
got to let him know how I feel
braving danger and roads in the dark-
got to let him know my love is real

forsaking my fears and forceful heartbeats-
got to state my feelings in a letter
brushing away tears to reach his door or mailbox-
he's got to know things can be better

pressing back home to safety on Piedmont
I really need to exhale
praying he reads with love and understanding
so that our relationship can excel

*Tangela Yvette Cooke*

# What if...

What if the man I used to love a lot
and the one I still consider a friend
should dare to try to peek into my life
better yet, try to get back in?

I have no regrets of yesteryear-
so I'd thank them for all the preparation
for a lasting, long-term relationship or
this new me plus you equation.

What if I met a man with a better car,
a better job and mounds of money-
who dared to sweep me off my feet
or tried to dip into your honey?

I would ask him, "Where were you before Mr. Right Now?"
Or I wouldn't give him the time of day,
because material things, status and money
don't matter much anyway...

What if... What if... There's no need for what ifs.
Your grass is green enough.
I'm content and I love the one I'm with
and if another wants me, tough.

# Pundit's Playground

*Learning without wisdom is a load of books on a donkey's back.*
-Zora Neale Hurston

# Living the Dream

I see color
but it's insignificant
character has
more meaning

I see groups,
families and classes
but it's not important
individuality and uniqueness
is what sets us apart
and thus
gets my attention.

I've witnessed
and was an object of
prejudice, racism
and discrimination
but I'd rather
testify about love.

That's just the way I see things.

*Tangela Yvette Cooke*

# Forget About the Funeral

If you love me, tell me now.
Recite my eulogy.
If you honor the way I live my life,
then share your joy with me.

If I've done something to make you proud
will you please let me know?
If I've done something to hurt you
confront me now or let it go.

If you miss me or want to see me,
call, write or just come over
and if you desire to express your love ...
do it while you're sober.

If you want to give me flowers - great.
I can utilize my senses.
If you want to express heart-felt words,
let's talk - don't put up fences.

If you want to spend more quality time
mark your calendar, it's a date.
If you want to celebrate the here and now,
know that tomorrow is much too late.

Please don't wait until my funeral
to pay your last respects.
Don't let a final, dormant cause
have an awakening effect.

# I Think Very Deeply: Processing

Are my ideas my own
or are they something that I've seen or heard
via one medium or another?

Did I really create, manufacture or develop
the finished product?

Are my words my own
or did I paraphrase, revise, recycle, steal or plagiarize
another's original expression?

The words that I write -
were they printed centuries ago or
are they being written right now
across different continents and
in different languages?

Is it dé jà vu?
Because sometimes I hear others
say and read what others
have written
and I know their words were mine.

Is this author's creative expressions
original and authentic or archaic?

Are my thoughts my own?

...

# I Think Very Deeply: Deprogramming

I had to
turn off my television and sound system
and tune into to me,
stop reading fiction
and focus on my reality,
cast aside cliches, quotes, and catchy phrases
and concentrate on my consciousness,
cease my exchanges on the phone
and gauge my experiences,
cover my ears, close my eyes
and go to my corner
so that I could think.

My mind is not a blank slate.
My mind is neither a recorder, nor a sponge.

I had to
dehypnoptize and reeducate myself,
trust my intuition,
conceptualize and implement common sense,
recapitulate and filter out
everything that I've learned or have been taught
through education and experience,
wake up, discover the truth,
and find my own proof
so that I could be free to think...

My mind is a maze of information.
My mind is both a vacuum and a vessel for knowledge.

My thoughts are my own.

## MY LOCKS

If my hair was meant to be straight,
it would have grown that way.
So I delivered it from chemicals
and true to nature it'll stay.

Now my head dons a regal crown –
a liberation of coils and kinks.
I'm genuinely happy to be nappy,
more so, free to think.

No longer influenced by the media
or it's European projections of beauty.
I've made celebrating my hairitage
my afro centric duty.

My locks are an extension of me-
a liberation of curls and kinks.
My locks are clean, down-to-earth and strong-
honoring the way I think.

So don't misname them or *dread* them,
'cause *dreadful* they're not.
Embrace my versatile, good, natural hair
or my free-style Nubian locks.

*Tangela Yvette Cooke*

# Quality Time

It was not the typical lover's rendezvous.
He was able to see me with his eyes
and not with his hands.
He unplugged his auditory senses
and listened with his heart.
I was in Paris and
we almost spent forever in each moment
of our time together.
I was taken aback
but we both left
fulfilled.

# Mirror, Mirror

I fell in love
with the most beautiful woman
ever.
She has a brilliant smile
and an amazing personality.
I love her long, naturally styled hair,
bright smile,
almond shaped eyes,
and dark brown skin.
I love this woman so much
that if I could be anyone else,
I'd choose not to be.
I'm mesmerized
by her internal and external beauty.
To see her everyday is a blessing.
I fell in love with me.

# Love AT LARJ
*dedicated to Linda, Arnita, Ronnie and Joseph*

Before him,
there was you.
Prior to playmates and roommates
you were my confidant too.

Connected by blood,
we share DNA.
Through breakups and fall out
our bond will stay.

Despite love, animosity
or separation,
I can depend on you-
my rock and consolation.

When distance and time
makes us estranged,
our history binds
the ties that remain.

You are the usurper of marriage
and so-called friends,
through divorce and desertion
you're there in the end.

Boyfriends and girlfriends
come and go,
but a sibling's love is constant.
This much I know.

# ArboREAL Experience
what my big brother taught me

When a fruitful branch
breaks from the family tree

It takes root
and creates a whole new entity

It remains its distance
and lets it former family be

*Tangela Yvette Cooke*

# Empirical

A friend told me that
many African-American parents
tend to grow up with their children
while white parents
watch their children grow up.

Where I come from this is true.

He also mentioned that
white parents
leave their children trusts when they die
while African-American parents
trust that their children won't get left behind.

In many instances they do.

He observed that some
African-American parents
discipline their children like masters punished slaves
while some white parents spare the rod
and allow their children to run free.

I confess, I've seen this too.

There are many truths and myths
about African-American and whites.
From hearsay, I've compared
and contrasted a few.
Think, reflect and open your eyes.
What have your observations shown you?

# Hello... Children First

If you do not plan
to have the very best
that life has to offer
and you choose
to live irresponsibly
not having anything
to proffer

Please don't include children in your purposeless life.

If unwanted pregnancies are results
of your lust, pleasure and
decisions not to use protection
and you're prolific
in this sexual aftermath
due to your serial
negligent election

Please make sure that your children feel loved upon arrival.

If you neglect
your child's health, hair and hygiene
and don't check on them
when they're not home
and try to pawn them off
on relatives
because you want to be alone

Please remember the golden rule when your children have to care for you.

If you're a selfish parent
with that old,
"welfare/project/trailer park/backwoods mentality"
and your life style
is a sight for
the Department of Children and Family Services
to see

Please get your act together, take care of your children and begin to live responsibly.

If you have to make sacrifices
to give your children
what they need
and you have to
defer your dreams
and make other plans
to succeed

Please remember that your children are worth it.

If you put your children first,
trust me,
God will make a way
and when you realize
that your life
is no longer about you
you'll see a better day-

Please recognize that children are gifts from God.

# Memory Lane

*Train a child in the way he should go,
and when he is old he will not turn from it.*
-Proverbs 22:6

# Autobio Poem – Age 15
*(January 10, 1985)*

Tangela
Reticent, Intelligent, Sensitive, and Fun-loving
Aunt of Katoiya, Darell and Takeisha
Lover of boys, food, and the Bill Cosby Show
Who feels proud when I achieve, mad when I don't get what I want and deprived because I'm not rich and famous
Who needs lots of money, plenty of happiness, and someone to pay for my college education
Who gives answers to my classmates, my father a challenge, and my nephews and nieces a playful time
Who fears failing anything, being killed, and not being rich in time to come
Who would like to see the man of my dreams, the world at peace, and a million dollars in my bank account, legally, tax-free, and with interest
Resident of Miami, Seventy-two Street
Cooke

*Tangela Yvette Cooke*

# All in the Opened Doors to the Future (1984)

The opened doors are increasing our views
Some of the jobs are fairly new
There is computer programming for us to do
There is teaching, accounting, and banking too

Outlooks and salaries for some jobs are great
But different jobs have certain pay

French and Spanish are languages we should learn
Because bilingual jobs are where the money is earned

The opened doors are getting wider and wider
Some jobs are offered to newcomers and outsiders

More knowledge and salary are just part of the deal
Because opportunities await all people with skills

# Autobio Poem – Age 17
*(October 8, 1986)*

Tangela
Intelligent, Cheerful, Ambitious, and Honest
Sister of Linda, Ronnie and Arnita
Lover of television, radio, and magazines
Who feels proud when I achieve, bored when I'm alone, and mad when I fail
Who needs a job, a long vacation, and a schedule change
Who gives help to my little brother, Joe, advice to my friends, and money to the poor
Who fears death, hurricanes, and scary movies
Who would like to see a black president, freedom in South Africa, and unity among all people
Resident of Miami, 72 Street
Cooke

# Just Say No! (1987)

### Diamante

Depressant
Harmful, addictive
Exhausting, intoxicating, inducing
Alcohol, sleeping pills, caffeine, nicotine
Wakening, exciting, arousing
Cancerous, poisonous
Stimulants

### Cinquain

Some drugs
make you feel glad.
Others make you feel sad.
But illegal drugs are bad.
Say no!

### Haiku

She tried the drug crack.
It had a great addiction.
She died that same year.

Just Say No!

# Forecast (1989)

A clear day don't matter much
When it's raining inside
Your inner sky is blue
with a waning internal ray
and an unyielding overcast
of the darkest black and gray
Followed by salty showers
Caused by a flood of depression
And multiple clouds of dismay
That not even sunshine can take away
But when you're content
Even on a stormy day
You know Roy G. Biv
Is not far away
But if you're sad
When the morning star abounds
It may as well go down
Because the sun don't matter much
If it's raining inside

# Home Sweet Home

*As I live and learn, inside I burn with emotions I would not dare to leak. Yet as I learn to live, I learn to give these emotions breath… so I speak.*
-Curtis L. Jones

# To a Woman's Heart

I ate kiwi,
but I thought about strawberries and watermelon.
I bit into an apple,
but I thought about strawberries and watermelon.
I sipped green tea,
but I was reminded of blended and juiced wheat grass, seaweed,
spirulina and at least five other organic fruits.

A womb... the fetus
may distinguish a woman/female from a man/male,
but our stomachs are analogous parts
to which you've reached my heart.

And my mind can't stop thinking about
Curty-Curt's yummy Strawberries and watermelon
and that very green beverage.

*Tangela Yvette Cooke*

# The Take Off

I swayed to the sounds
On the runway
Just before he swept me
Off my feet.

There was a bump
During the flight,
But I still enjoyed
The ride.

And like an answer to
A prayerful song,
He picked my spirits up.

# Prolific

Ever since
You penetrated my Soul
I was impregnated with verse
And I'm craving-
Can't stop craving-
Can't quench my thirst
For another taste
Of Soulrebral satisfaction.

You've created,
No, we've created
Life
From what seems like a swim upstream
From the 17th through the 21st
When your art emerged from your head
Onto the surface
To state was said,
And it filled her up on the 22nd
Causing multiple orgasms.

The first hit fertilized phenomenally.
Was it just a hit…
Cause he didn't miss and will he strike to win…
Or was it a routine one write stand
Or will you be The Man and not just a man
And whip out your pen again.

Tangela Yvette Cooke

# Kismet

Finally, I've met a man
Who's dared to make love to my mind

I was skillfully deflowered
By verse, imagery and rhyme

And I reached an orgasm
Of a different kind

…

You, man, have managed
To touch my soul

Forget wasting words,
To be Curt is bold

I'm still feeling spasms
Though my flesh is on hold

…

A beautiful Blaq man
With an infectious smile

Revealed to me symptoms
Of deep-seated denial

Of truth, the Blaqwhole
And the Azuso's trial

...

This mind-blowing encounter
Your Soul's expressions

Is proof that our acquaintance
Is one of the Creator's blessings

And you've satisfied my mind and Soul...
yet my spiritual climax has no cessation.

*Tangela Yvette Cooke*

# Her Written Soliloquy

In a short period
Or just immeasurable time
We've shared the same space
And you've saturated my mind.

Yesterday,
I couldn't stop thinking of Curt
And how maybe, just maybe
I've captured the wind.
Perhaps maybe this time
I've reached my search's end.

It's a challenge
Being the women that I've become.
I feel hard and I think hard.
I'm an enigma to some.

Today,
I can't stop thinking about Curt
Maybe he's preventive medicine
for a broken spirit.
Perhaps maybe this time
I just might hear it.

I have another incentive
to preserve my youth.
And I ask, "Will we partner
In the search for the truth?

Instinctively,
I rhetorically query,
"Is it worth it to
Go on umpteen Soul dates,
Unlock and open up my Soul's gate,
Pay insurmountable Soul rates
By serving up my Soul on an invisible plate
To resolve if I've found my Soul mate?"

Tomorrow,
May delude me.
But time will tell.

# SM

You can say
That the perfect man for me, Curtis,
My Soul mate
Was being created for me over a period of
28 years,
But his model (image)
Was engrained in my Soul
Ever since I had a Soul.

SM Phase I
My first love and definition of beauty or
The best qualities of my dad:
Dark, handsome, bold, fierce, charming, youthful
And just the beginning

SM Phase II
My second "love" and first serious relationship
Containing attributes that I adored in a boyfriend:
Tall, athletic, playful, boyish, poetic, loving
And a man in the making

SM Phase III
My third "love" and second serious union
Including characteristics that I admired in a man:
Intelligent, forthright, a gentleman, witty, insightful, no-nonsense
Close but not quite there

SM Final Phase
My true love and potentially the Final Product
Who encompasses everything I want in a man
From SM Phase I through SM Phase III and
With finesse adds Soul and/or spirituality, passion, romance and
Commitment and all that is needed to complete
The SM prototype that has been engrained
In my Soul, ever since I had a Soul.

You can say that each phase of
My life slowly but surely
Introduced and prepared me
For the one true love of my life and
I can clearly see, hear, feel, smell and taste
Curtis, my Soul mate.

*Tangela Yvette Cooke*

# Untitled

You know I love you
Because I love myself.

I see me in you.

In another dimension
You would be Tangelo
And I would be Curtesia.

You know we're not lost
Because we found each other.

We were each other's prize at the end of a maze.

In wonderland
You would be the King, and I, the Queen
Of Hearts.

# My Soul's Creation

My Soul
Exposed
Its
Cognitive underlying rationale through it's imaginative subconsciousness
And gave my mate a name-
Curtis.

My Soul
Conjured up a relationship translating imagery and senses
Into reality
Or a real man-
Curtis.

For a moment in time I dated Curtis.

Unfortunately,
My Soul also revealed
And I discovered
That our courtship
Was surreal.

CURTIS, CURTIS... I glimpsed at my future with Curtis,
A beautiful hologram or materialized figment
Of my imagination.

Maybe next time
My Soul will not delude me.

Maybe at the right time
My Soul will choose a mate
And he will be mortal, for real, tangible
And like the Soul-
Forever.

# Dead End

## featuring poems by Michael S. Litwhiler
## inspired by the study of Tycology

*He who forgives ends the quarrel.*
-African Proverb

# Hurricane T (ending in A) (1987)

It was a muggy, wet morning
when his life passed him by.
Throughout those remorseful few days
all he could do was cry.

All he had built up,
all he had made strong,
was torn down by her forceful winds
due to all that he had done wrong

*Tangela Yvette Cooke*

# You're Right (1988)

A man
sometimes the blindest creature
A woman
mostly his brightest feature
His best friend
His solo informer
Unafraid to back into
a corner

The lover
willing to exceed the limit
The fighter
knocked down, but not knocked out
The fool destined
to shout and pout
Prime introducer of doubt

Yes Mr. Parker Love's Gonna Get me
But woman don't forget me
As you walk off into the dark night
Baby, oh yes – you're right.

# Innocent Brown Goddess (1997)

I know you
I see you
I chase you
through vibrant, late summer fields
Your beautiful brown skin contrasts
the light beige hay
Laughter exits your strong lips
You have nothing to hide
I don't know what I'm chasing – your laughter or your countenance
You have no guilt of self-presence
Your warm, smooth skin
creates a graceful path for
the water of the brook
beneath the sparkling waterfall
You capture my body
with my eyes
You are exciting nature
Men fear your beauty
but your mind is strong
you know how to keep in check
What is to some women self-poison
is to you a pleasant gift from him
but not at all the Soul of you
Beneath your calcium frame
lies an amazingly well balanced being
As I stand in the brook
filled with emotion, I too fear
your beauty, your whole beauty
Your water moistened cloth skirt
clings to your twisting body
You are full of femininity
I cannot help to desire
to hold this beautiful creature in me
I want you to feel my respect for you
to feel my desire to know you
Laugh my queen. Laugh
How beautiful it is, your smile
Your joy penetrates my Soul
My fingers long to caress the line

*Tangela Yvette Cooke*

that runs up your back
Yes my lips desire to rub
passionately against yours
I do desire to taste your neck
To deny is to be dishonest
The warm sun splashes our wet bodies
with approval
Its brightness trickling along the
water
My strength embraces you
and you embrace my strength
as we stand in nature embraced
for now and forever

# (1998)

i feel down when my cookie feels down
i wish her smiles when I see her frown
i want to see her feeling so proud
i want to see her screaming it aloud
she has traveled a long hard road
she has held her hand while others simply fold
i ask her simply to keep playing her hand
keep her head high and firmly stand
at times I know this is asking a lot
but baby, one day your gonna hit the jackpot!!!!!
and if you like this poem think of your creative writing teacher
on presenting this with disgust, he may meet you
but in your heart you know it is true
all that matters is what it means to you
the lesson is don't let others stand in your way
if its true to your heart, then it's o.k.
and sometimes when you feel like a rookie
just remember we love you cookie

Tangela Yvette Cooke

## (2002)

once upon a time i sat in an exotic place
a time i look back at without disgrace
i wore oxfords and tight jean pants
different paths i crossed from my former peers
they never once felt my kinds of fears
they never once cried my kinds of tears
not once did they know the things i knew
they never felt that growth that i grew
not once did those northern boys see a roach
those conservative boys never even smoked one
but i did in a place so far away
when my folks told me this was not okay
i saw gigantic palms lace the pink urban sky
in my youth i may have thought i could fly
here i sit pondering of those glory days
my life now seems in such a haze
but i know i will get by no matter what
no matter what i have not one regret
i'm gonna keep on livin' to the fullest on that you can bet

## Sober Poetry (2003)

this god damned bottle, this pint, this shot glass
this good woman leaving this valuable time passed
you've had me for many years, now your getting the boot
i'm giving you the door without one final salute
you were suppose to make me happy, take away the pain
you were supposed to ease my mind when i thought i was going insane
the insecurity, the pressure, the guilt and the sorrow
the lack of responsibility and the constant need to borrow
but together we have just multiplied what was already there
i'm tired, broken, worn but somehow still care
now it's a chance at life or a choice of death
another drink of poison or a first fresh breath
i want my mind back and i want my heart back too
so i'm taking it back, taking it back from you

## About the Author

A native of Florida, Tangela Yvette Cooke is the author of *Tangible Times* and an aspiring performance poet. She lives and still writes in Atlanta, Georgia.